T0157568

Jesus Does a Body Good

Annette Bailey

iUniverse, Inc.
Bloomington

Jesus Does a Body Good

iUniverse books may be ordered through booksellers or by contacting:

iUniverse
1663 Liberty Drive
Bloomington, IN 47403
www.iuniverse.com
1-800-Authors (1-800-288-4677)

ISBN: 978-1-4697-9554-6 (sc)
ISBN: 978-1-4697-9555-3 (e)

Library of Congress Control Number: 2012904484

Printed in the United States of America

iUniverse rev. date: 5/18/2012

I would like to acknowledge first God for putting in my heart to write about hurting people. Men, women and children that are going through things that only God knows. I would like people to know that the little kids God gave them are special and God has a purpose for each one of them. They have to know that they are special, wanted and loved. The things I went through made me a better person and with God in my life it's like a new beginning.

I know reading the words will change hearts and change families.

I want this book of poems to bless people everywhere.

Husband

For when God sent you to me. He sent the precise example of what a husband should be. You are my hero, a gentleman in every respect. Our marriage was ordained in heaven. It was sealed with the heavenly angels rejoicing, with the blessings of God and family. God loves you, and he sees the sacrifice. The things close to your heart. You have been a strong tower, inspiration to all. Quietly good that is what makes you who you are. You never give up on any situation, standing on God's word. We have been through the good times and the bad. We've seen God bring us out with his almighty hands. Chosen by God to carry his word. Souls are dying. They are waiting just for you. You hold the key, come forth and set the captives free. A vessel set aside for the master's use, so tell them wherever you go. God is everlasting, his peace will abide. All he asking of each one of us is to believe with our heart that he is the true and living God.

Broken Hearts

Children are special to God. Why treat them this way? That baby never had a chance to say "Mom, I will make you proud of me some day?" The father that never had time for his children because of another woman. The mother that said "I wish you were never born." The choosing of one brother over another. The beating that they didn't deserve. Oh, the broken hearts. Love your children. Give them a chance. God gave them to you. The love of many may have waxed cold. Can you hear the voices of the little children? Please listen to each one for they are so alone each ones little eyes tell a story. Love them for evermore. Give them a chance to grow and be what God called them to be. No more broken hearts.

Remember To

Hug your children when they come home from school. Always tell them that they are somebody. Teach your children good manners. Be their role model. Never stop loving them. Be there for your children. Put God first. Be the best Mom and Dad you can be. Pray before they leave home for school. Tell them they are the best. Children are somebody.

Habits to Follow

Prayer. Reading the word. Walking in the word. Intercessory prayer for loved ones. Having faith in God. Asking God what his will is for you. Use knowledge and wisdom. Be joyful, live holy and to forgive.

Lonely Heart

A little girl waits by the window lonely and cold. The fear, uncertainty, not understanding at all. As she waited by the window, there is silence all around. You can only hear the patter of little feet making the sounds. Christmas is rapidly approaching, excitement is in the air. For in this house there is no love, no one to care. She longs for Mom and Dad to love her just a simple hug or even a little kiss. As she listens to the carols outside, she heard the children singing, giving God the glory exhorting the King of Kings! She heard about how special she was and the goodness of God. His love had reached a little girl and mended her broken heart. Oh, the happiness, the peace and contentment within. At last she knew Jesus loved her and how excited she was. Mom and Dad came home and saw her little face was all aglow. She told them about Jesus and how he loved her so. The greatest gift on that Christmas day was the gift of love. They will tell the story wherever they go. Praising God for who he is. Thankful that he let them see how special and precious a little girl can be. Don't forget three important words- I love you. Let your children know you care.

Thank You God

Hello, God. What a brand new day? Thank you for waking me up today. Thank you for life today. Thank you for Mother and Daddy. My brother and sisters who love me so dear. The food we eat sent from God above. Dear, God we thank you for the love.

In Time of Trouble

Sometimes we do not know what to do. We cry and our hearts get heavy and the answer never comes as fast as we want it to. He hears every prayer, and sees us every day. Remember that help is on the way. The little birds get up every morning and fly away knowing that everything is taken care of that very day. Don't worry you just stand still and watch him work every prayer answered, and every request met. What an awesome God and he has not failed yet. Be encouraged!

Children

Children are a blessing from above, so treat them special with lots of love. Each unique in his own way and one may be President someday. They are a reflection of each one of us. Be glad that God left them in our trust. Love, guidance, and prayer everyday it will go along with them along the way. Tell them God's love stands when everything else falls. Building a bond that surpasses all. Make them and mold them into who they should be and tell them to keep God in the center of the family tree.

He Cares

Sometimes it may seem that no one cares for you. Nothing you seem to do ever come through but, oh how God cares for you and me. He left Heaven came down to give his life for ransom. Never said a word, a love that is overflowing reaches out every day. Leave it to him, he will find a way. Let him come into your heart and stay. He will bring peace, joy, happiness, and a willingness to live. No matter what, try Jesus and never let him go and watch him love you for evermore.

Never Give Up

Never give up on any situation no matter how it looks or how it seems. God promises peace in the midst of the storm, peace that will guide you. God will lift you up with his almighty hands. He will send angels to comfort and surround you with love. He will be a doctor and a lawyer. Whatever you want him to be don't give up because he loves us one and all. Remember he cares. He will see you through. Give God the glory for he is the **Great I Am**. The problem is not big enough that God cannot solve. Praise him for being **Almighty God**.

Lonely Hearts

Sometime we cannot see the lonely hearts children carry every day. The hurt, uncertainty, and the fear. Things they don't understand like grownups do. If we take a little time to let them know we care. A simple I love you, patience when they make a mistake, like most of us do. Mother and Daddy waiting with a big hug when they come home from school. Things they look forward to. God has lent them to us for only a short time to be the best parents. Love them every day. Remember, you are the first role model that shapes them the very first day.

I Can

I can be everything God said I could be. He never lies. His word holds true. You are victorious in everything you do. Hold your head up high. Walk in prosperity every day. God gave his life for each one of us. His words we can surely trust. I can serve him with joy and peace, knowing every problem is solved. Every situation is under control. Remember wherever you go, be what God wants you to be. Because he gave his life, love and Heaven-Eternity. That is why we can walk free.

What is an Usher?

We praise God for you are special doing a job for God and not
for man. We praise him for your dedication, ushering God's
people in one by one. Because his word compelled them to come.
Always be patient putting attitudes aside. A smile, a how are you
today? Can start each person on their way. It is honored by God,
esteemed from on high. The Master always has need for you and
I. We praise him for who he is. The Great I Am brought us out of
darkness into the marvelous light. Be the best usher God called
you to be. Let the Holy Ghost shine through you. Automatically
people will see Jesus in each one of you.

God's Best

God sent his best to you and I, his son the precious Lamb from on high. To take away sin he bled and died. He is the beginning and the end. He will be lawyer, peacemaker, and daddy – whatever you want. Trust him. Love him. Rest in his peace. Give God the glory and praise him every day. Without him, there is no other way. Never forget where God brought you from. He is the best.

Be Glad

No matter what you are going through remember God truly loves you. He died so that we could live again. Rose in victory for every man, woman, boy and girl. Be glad a love that has stood the test of time. He specializes in mending broken hearts. Doing the impossible, no one else can do. He came to restore and make the burden light. The battle is all ready won. Praise God and be glad he is working it out on your behalf.

Who is God?

God created each one of you to love him, to praise him, to be part of your life. He cares for you to tell of his goodness wherever you go. To be the light for others to see. He came to show us a better way. Be glad he died for you and I. He created man in the image of himself, the greatest gift of all. He laid down his life for you and I. He will take care of you. Love him with all your heart- come out of sin. Begin a new life that God has planned since the beginning of time. Find out who he is. Give God a chance.

Peace

Peace in the world is being kind to others every day. Smile as you pass someone along the way. Peace is respecting every race, color and creed. Helping others when they have a need. Peace with all men, women, boys and girls is what God would have us to be and live in a country where we are all free. Peace is what will hold this country together. It is which way the world will go and it will never fail. If we walk in the peace that God has called.

Special

You are special in every way. A kind husband that no one can compare. You are everything a husband should be. A special blessing that God has given me.

Almighty

God is almighty. God is true. Remember he loves each one of you.

Oh, Taste and See

Oh, taste and see that the Lord is good. He came down to redeem man back again. The chains of bondage were broken. The captive set free. What a mighty God. For he is the master builder specializing in mending broken hearts. He called us out of darkness into the marvelous light. Vessels set aside for the Master's use to carry God's word and stand for the truth. His grace is sufficient. His peace flows from everlasting to everlasting. He is that solid rock in the midst of the storm. He is the beginning and end. Wait on him, never give up, trust him, and love him. Rest in the word- every prayer will be answered. Every request met. He is an awesome God and has not failed yet. No greater love, No greater love the heavenly Father could give. So taste and see that the Lord is good.

A World of Peace

Brothers and sisters united in love, understanding one another. Never accept defeat, rising above all adversity, and having a sense of pride. Laying aside the past, looking to the future. God must be first priority, that is where it all began. Being proud of who we are. The chains of bondage were broken when God shed his innocent blood. Therefore, man is no longer bound. Peace is teaching our little ones from generation to generation to proclaim Jesus as their Lord and Savior, the Almighty God. Tell them his grace is sufficient, that his peace flows everlasting to everlasting. Peace is getting a hold of the Horn of the Alter. Praying until a change comes. It is hope, determination, a willingness to go on and never forgetting where God has brought each one of us from.

Woman of God

WOMAN of righteous distinction, called by God into the beauty of holiness. Vessel set aside for the Master's use. Carrying God's word and standing for the truth. You are a gift from God precious in his sight. Sent to draw others into his marvelous light. Woman come forth, tell lost souls of me. How nothing but the word can set them free. O' take heed to what God tells you to do and work in that gift he has given you.

Souls of Men

The souls of men and women are dying every day. Each one precious, they just need someone to show them a better way. If we take time to show love that truly comes from the heart. It will reach others and give them a brand new start. God's love came to set the captives free. To make men forever and ever withhold, walking upright with dignity. Remember when you see someone down and out. Give them a hand and tell them what God's love is all about.

Marriage

Marriage is ordained by God. It is when two people come together as one with God as the center. Being considerate of one another. Uplifting one another in times of trouble. Being there for each other in good times as well as bad times. Asking God's decision on every matter that may arise. Being the best wife and/or husband that you can be. Always keep a neat and tidy home. Keep your appearance the same as when you were dating. Give each other a kiss when you come home from work. Never criticizing each other in public. Make your spouse the number one person in your life next to God. Always respect each other and let no one come between your marriage. Take time for each other. Work at your marriage. Keep your business at home and between yourselves. Husband treat your wife like a Queen, little things mean a lot. Wife treats your husband like a King, uplifting and supporting him in all his deeds. Always put God first in your lives. Remember together you stand, divided you fall.

Happiness

Happiness is seeing God blessing his people every day. His goodness that wakes us up and start each one on his way. Knowing God's angels will watch over us letting no hurt or harm come our way. Happiness is walking in the peace of God. He will never leave or forsake you .He is calling. For men, woman, boys and girls to worship him with a true heart. He loves you.

Pastor's Wife

You are the apple of God's eyes. He holds a special love for you. You are a light to those that are weak. Dedication to the man of God. You love God with all of your heart. He sees the sacrifice and he knows. A role model of what a Pastor's wife should be. Full of knowledge you will lift up a standard no matter what. A boldness that has stood the test of time. For you are special to God. God sends all his love for he called you to be. The woman of the hour, by your husband's side. To walk in the beauty of holiness. Where God's precious love abides.

What is a Father

Father's are strong towers told to never ever cry. They are loving, kind, powerful as can be. The center of the family. Providing and taking care of every need. A true father will lead his children in the way as they should go. Stand by his wife forever most. They are to be respected; a role model for boy's and girl's to see. Walking upright, putting God first in every decision. Being the best father God called them to be, and that special father for the world to see.

The Meaning of Easter

Christ died on the cross for you and I. He came to redeem man back again. He took 39 stripes for our healing. Shed his innocent blood. He rose on this very day, victorious with all power in his hands. What a mighty God he is. That is what Easter is all about. It is not buying a new dress, Easter eggs, candy bunnies, coming to church showing off outfits. Coming only on Easter to see what everyone is wearing on that day. In other words giving only one Sunday a year to the Lord. Somewhere we have lost the true meaning of Easter. Remember put Christ first not only on Easter but every day. Celebrate Easter with Christ as Lord.

Looking In What Do You See?

Looking in the word what do you see? Do you see all the good things he provided for his people? His benefits, covenant, love and all the promises. In the word we have all the tools to live a clean Christian life. We see the faithfulness of God. The wisdom and the knowledge. The word can change your life for the best. He promised a new Heaven and Earth. Praise God. Do you see the joy, mercy, forgiveness, healing. Truly God Cares.

Hebrews 10:23 "Let us hold fast the profession of our faith, without wavering for he is faithful that promised." Looking in the word what do you see?